JOHN MAYER
BATTLE STUDIES

This book was approved by John Mayer

Photography by Albert Watson

Transcribed by Jeff Jacobson

Cherry Lane Music Company
Director of Publications/Project Editor: Mark Phillips
Project Coordinator: Rebecca Skidmore

ISBN 978-1-60378-231-9

Visit our website at www.cherrylaneprint.com

JOHN MAYER BATTLE STUDIES

Immediately following the release of John Mayer's Battle Studies, the buzz began that the seven-time Grammy-winning artist had another bulletproof hit on his hands. "*Billboard Top 200 Chart*" confirmed that Battle Studies, Mayer's fourth studio album, reached the highest chart position in the U.S. after a release week that catered to fans and focused on performance. *Billboard* magazine called *Battle Studies* "the best and most adventurous of his four studio albums."

Battle Studies incorporates the warmth, melodies, and simplicity of '70s and '80s California rock and pop. The album is a confessional, relaxed, and liberated album recorded in a private home in California, where Mayer lived and worked over the course of six months before wrapping at the famed Capitol Studios in Los Angeles. The album was co-produced by Mayer and Steve Jordan and released in November 2009 by Columbia Records.

Since his acclaimed debut in 2001, with *Room for Squares*, each release has earned Mayer additional accolades. Through 2003's *Heavier Things*, his work with John Mayer Trio in 2005, 2006's *Continuum*, and now, *Battle Studies*, Mayer has established himself as a musician and collaborator who exceeds genre boundaries. The guitarist, vocalist, and songwriter has earned seven Grammy Awards and sold over 12 million albums worldwide.

In May 2007 *Time* magazine placed Mayer on their "*Time* 100" list of the most influential contemporary thinkers, leaders, artists, and entertainers. For two consecutive years, *Rolling Stone* magazine featured Mayer on the cover of their annual "Guitar" issue—first with the May 2008 "Living Guitar Legends" issue and then as part of February 2007's "Guitar Heroes" roundup, showcasing Mayer with peers and icons alike.

Pairings with a range of artists is a defining trait of the musician whose collaborative streak is well known. From rock to blues, hip-hop to jazz to country, Mayer has performed and/or recorded with Eric Clapton, B.B. King, Buddy Guy, T-Bone Burnett, Herbie Hancock, the Dixie Chicks, Jay Z, Alicia Keys, and Taylor Swift. In 2005 Mayer famously toured and recorded with power players Pino Palladino and Steve Jordan as John Mayer Trio, whose live album, Try!, featured searing blues and rock.

As on *Continuum*, Mayer again took the helm as the co-producer of *Battle Studies* and crafted what is arguably one of the best rock albums of this century. The consistency with which Mayer combines word craft and melody has earned him rarefied status in popular culture as a genuine and respected songwriter and musician.

CONTENTS

HEARTBREAK WARFARE

Words and Music by
John Mayer

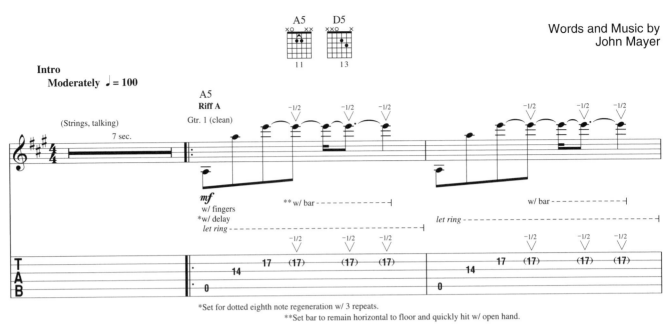

*Set for dotted eighth note regeneration w/ 3 repeats.

**Set bar to remain horizontal to floor and quickly hit w/ open hand.

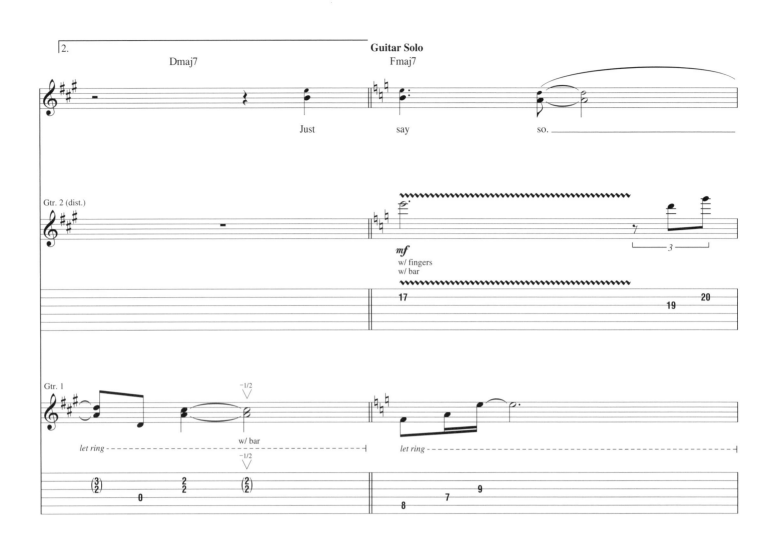

Just say so. _____

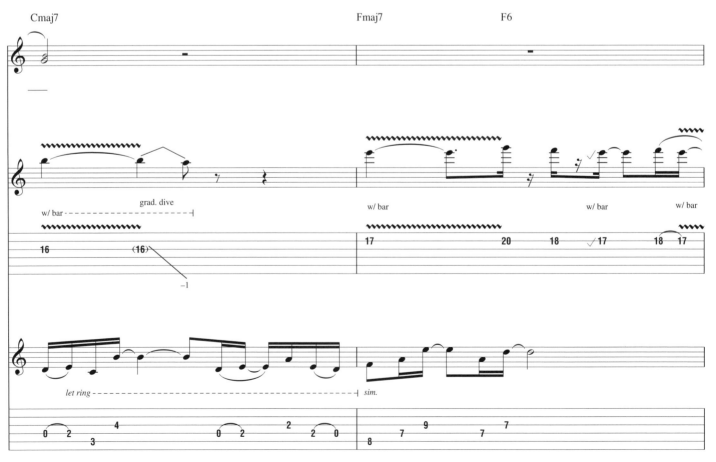

How come the on - ly way to know _____ how high _____ you get me _____ is to

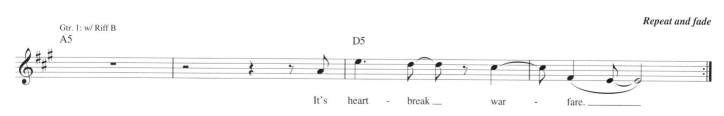

ALL WE EVER DO IS SAY GOODBYE

Words and Music by
John Mayer

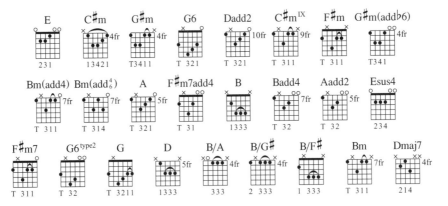

Tune down 1/2 step:
(low to high) Eb-Ab-Db-Gb-Bb-Eb

Verse
Moderately slow ♩ = 64

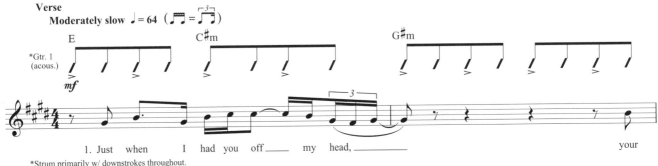

*Gtr. 1 (acous.)

mf

1. Just when I had you off ___ my head, ___ your

*Strum primarily w/ downstrokes throughout.

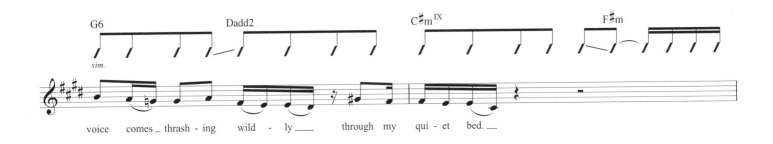

sim.

voice comes ___ thrash-ing wild-ly ___ through my qui-et bed. ___

Rhy. Fig. 1

You say you want to try ___ a-gain, ___ but I've ___

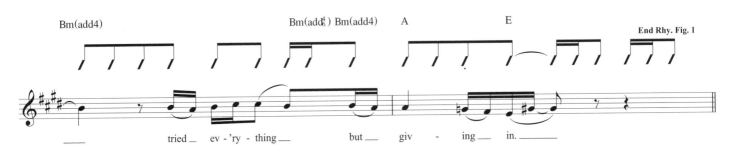

End Rhy. Fig. 1

___ tried ___ ev-'ry-thing ___ but ___ giv-ing ___ in.

2. I bought a tick-et on ____ a plane, _____ and

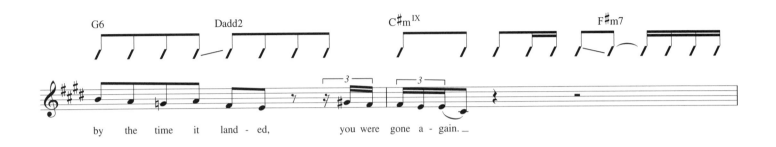

by the time it land-ed, you were gone a-gain. ____

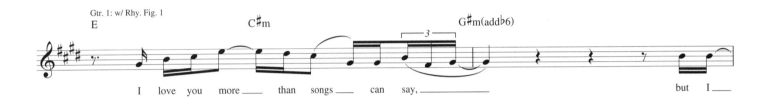

I love you more ____ than songs ____ can say, _____ but I ____

D.S. al Coda

____ can't keep a-run-ning af - ter yes-ter-day. ____ So...

We say ____ good - bye. ____ We say ____

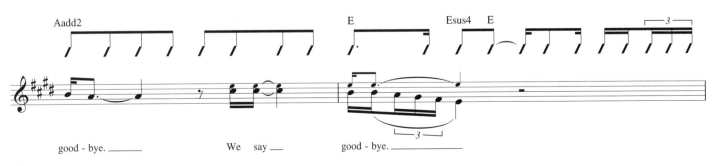

good - bye. ____ We say ____ good - bye. ____

Guitar Solo

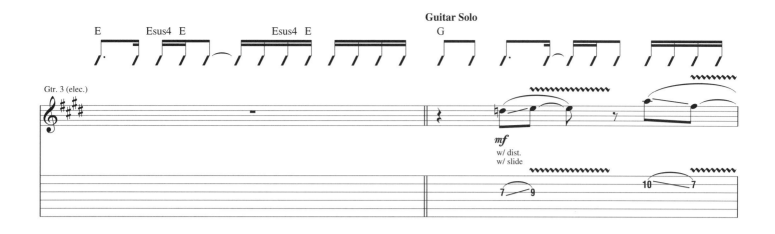

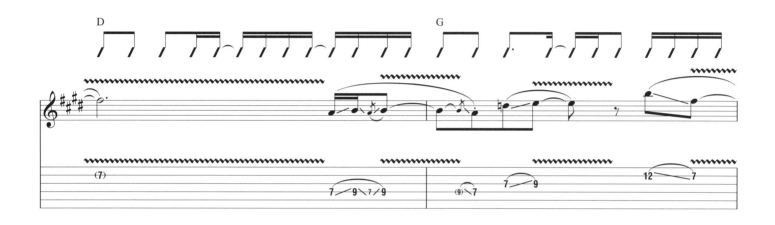

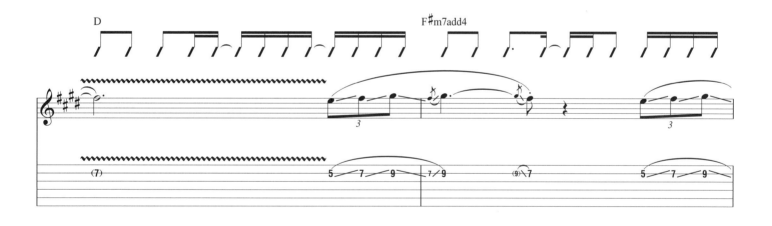

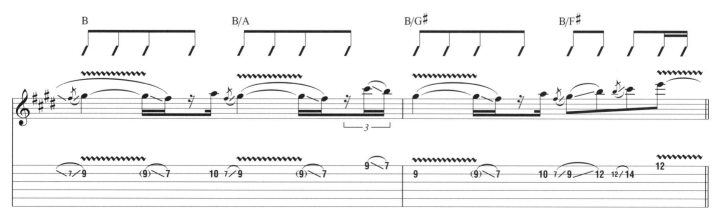

HALF OF MY HEART

Words and Music by
John Mayer

Verse

Gtr. 1: w/ Riff A (2 times)
1st time, Gtr. 3 tacet
2nd time, Gtr. 3: w/ Fill 1
Gtr. 4: w/ Rhy. Fig. 1 (2 times)

1. I was born _____ in the arms _____ of i - mag - i - nar - y _____
2. I was made _____ to be - lieve _____ I'd nev - er love _____ some - bod - y _____

*Chord symbols reflect basic harmony.

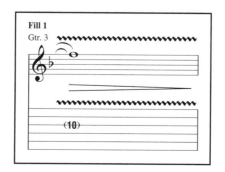

20

With half of my heart. _____

Your faith _

Bridge

Gtrs. 2 & 3 tacet

F   Am7   Cm7

Gtr. 4

Voc. Fig. 1

is strong ___ but I can on - ly fall short for so
(Ah.) ___

Gtr. 5 (elec.)

mf

w/ clean tone

*T

let ring

*T = Thumb on 6th string.

**Refers to upstemmed notes only.

Gm7   F   Am7

End Voc. Fig. 1

long.   Down the road, ___ lat - er on, ___ you will

let ring

T

Bkgd. Voc.: w/ Voc. Fig. 1

Gtr. 5 tacet

Cm7   Gm7   B♭

hate that I nev - er gave more to you ___ than half of my heart, ___

Gtr. 3

T

let ring

let ring

22

And half of my heart ___ is the heart ___ of a man ___ who's nev - er

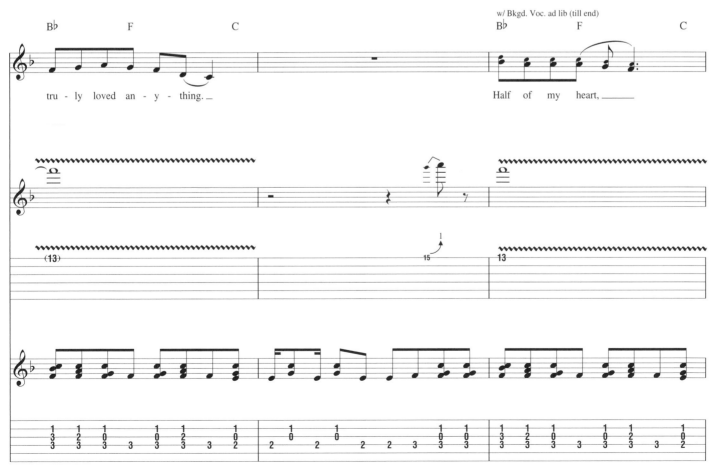

tru - ly loved an - y - thing. ___

Half of my heart, _____

TABS ♥   Search!   Advanced   + **Submit tab**

FRESH TABS | 0-9 A B C D E F G H I J K L M N O P Q R S T U V W X Y Z | TOP 100 TABS

+ **Submit review**
+ **Submit article**

print
send
report

Only A Womans Heart Chords

by **Mary Black tabs** | tabbed by **Unregistered** | **comments** (0)

2 votes

✔ **Only A Womans Heart Chords**

☑ **Highlight chords**   ☐ **Display chord diagrams**   **Transpose song**   [Down 2 Half Steps ◆] [Transpose]   AUTO Scroll

♫ Tab Pro |◀   ▶   ◀))   ▬▬   🎚   ◉   Ψ   ◉   Q ▬▬

Only A Womans Heart chords by Mary Black, www.Ultimate-Guitar.Co   [Like ◁ 422k]

💾 View Only A Womans Heart tab on your iPhone, iPod Touch or Android
   Listen to Only A Womans Heart
   Add to favourites
   Difficulty: novice

🎸 Can't play "Only A Womans Heart"? Improve your playing via easy step-by-step video lessons! 🎸   Help

```
Artist: Mary Black
Title: Only A Woman's Heart
chords by: pieofhshit@yahoo.com

Capo: 3rd Fret ( I find the 1st fret easier)
Chords G: 320033
       D: xx0232
       C: x32013
       Em:022003

Some embellishments on the chord changes are recomended
as it can be quite bland otherwise.
Simple descensions/ascensions should suffice
eg. C -> G
e --3-----3---
B --1-----3---
G --0-----0---
D --2-----0---
A --3-----2---
E --x-0-2-3---

Intro (fine)
G - D - C - D - G - D - C - D


(Chorus)
G            D       Em            C
My heart is low, my heart is so low
     G         D             Em - C - D
As only a woman's heart can be
       G         D        Em     C
As only a woman's, as only a woman's
       G         D          C - G
As only a woman's heart can know


(verse 1)
G                 D
The tears that drip
     Em           C
From my bewildered eyes
G         D            Em - C
Taste of bitter sweet romance
G                D - Em
You're still in my hopes
                 C    G
```

Only A Womans Heart Lyrics
by Mary Black Lyrics

```
                        You're still on my mind, oh
               D             Em        C - D
And even though I manage on my own


(Chorus)
G            D      Em            C
My heart is low, my heart is so low
    G      D                Em - C - D
As only a woman's heart can be
    G        D     Em        C
As only a woman's, as only a woman's
    G        D              C - G
As only a woman's heart can know


(verse 2)
G                   D
When restless eyes
     Em              C
Reveal my troubled soul
G          D         Em - C
And memories flood my weary heart
G                 D - Em
I mourn for my dreams
                    C     G
I mourn for my wasted love
          D            Em       C - D
And while I know that I'll survive alone



(Chorus)
G            D      Em            C
My heart is low, my heart is so low
    G      D                Em - C - D
As only a woman's heart can be
    G        D     Em        C
As only a woman's, as only a woman's
    G        D              C - G
As only a woman's heart can know


(Chorus to fade)
G            D      Em            C
My heart is low, my heart is so low
    G      D                Em - C - D
As only a woman's heart can be
    G        D     Em        C
As only a woman's, as only a woman's
    G        D              C - G
As only a woman's heart can know
```

🎸 **Can't play "Only A Womans Heart"? Improve your playing via easy step-by-step video lessons!** 🎸

UG plus: remove banner

WHO SAYS

Words and Music by
John Mayer

Moderately, in 2 ♩ = 92 **Verse**

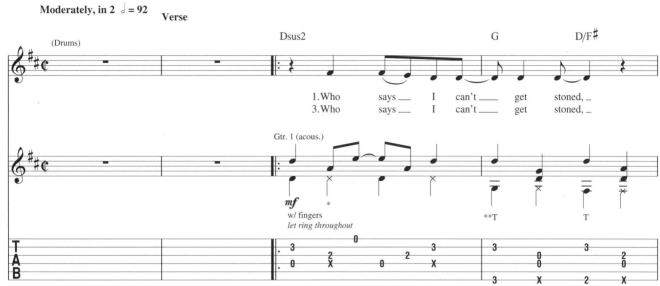

*Throughout song, execute beats 2 and 4 by hitting muted string w/ R.H.
thumb while simultaneously flicking in downward motion w/ index finger.

**T = Thumb on 6th string.

Cit - y.　　　It's been a long＿＿＿ night＿＿

*Pull off to bottom note while flicking top note.

＿ in ⎰ Bat - on　Rouge.＿＿
　　　 ⎱ Aus - tin,　too.＿＿

2nd time, Gtr. 1: w/ Rhy. Fill 2

I don't re - mem - ber＿＿＿ you look - ing an - y bet - ter.＿＿

Rhy. Fill 1
Gtr. 1

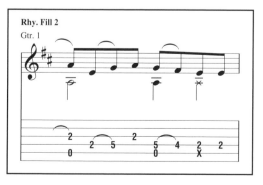

Rhy. Fill 2
Gtr. 1

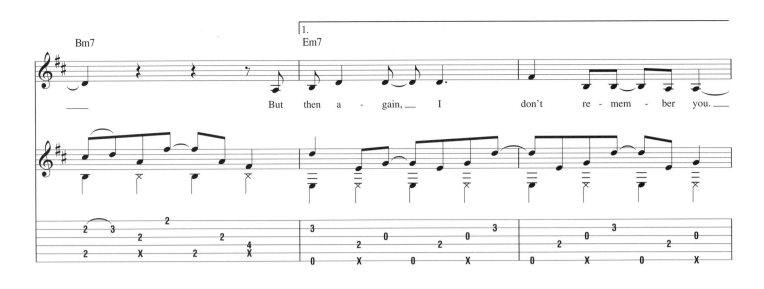

But then a - gain, ___ I don't re - mem - ber you. ___

then a - gain, ___ I don't re - mem - ber you. ___

Interlude

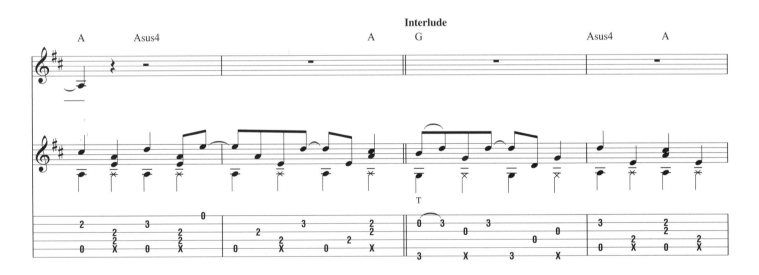

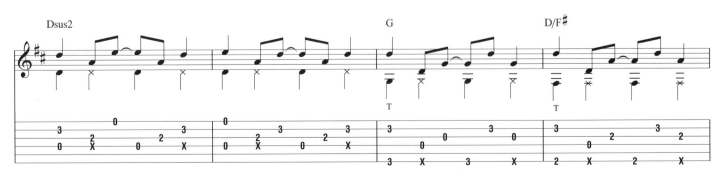

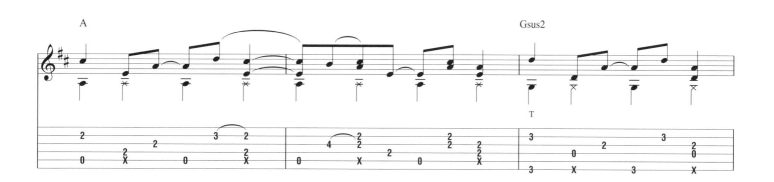

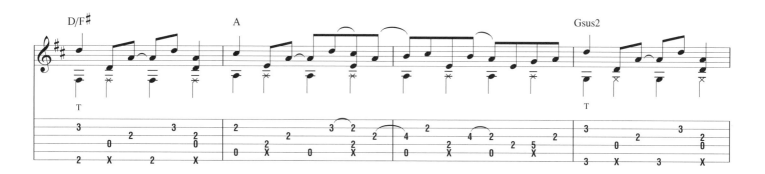

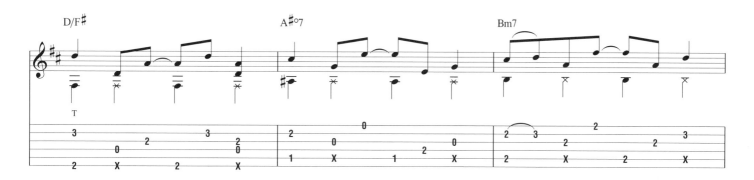

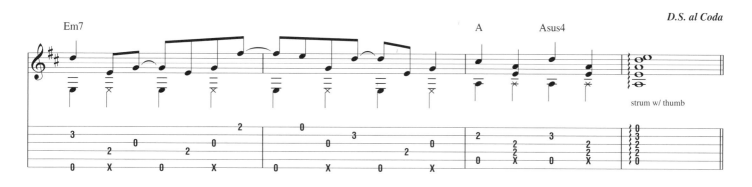

D.S. al Coda

strum w/ thumb

⊕ Coda

Mm. _____

It's been a long _____

then a - gain, ___ I don't re - mem - ber, don't re - mem - ber you. ___

Outro

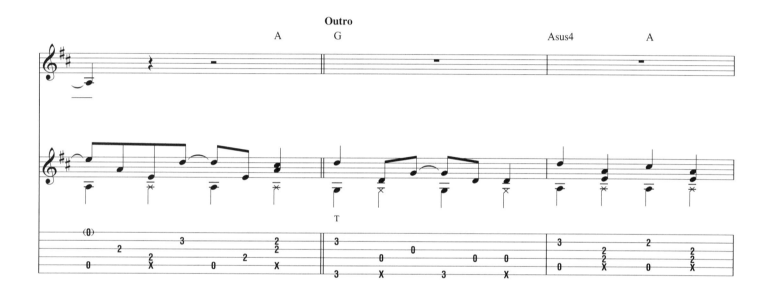

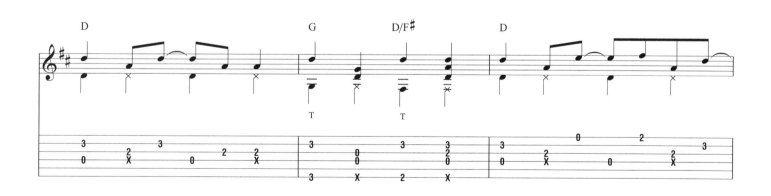

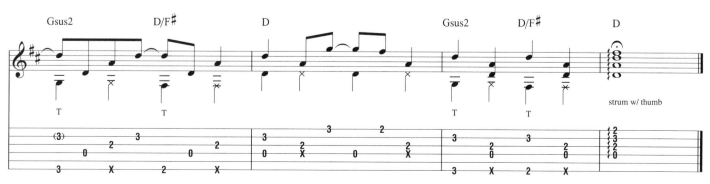

strum w/ thumb

PERFECTLY LONELY

Words and Music by
John Mayer

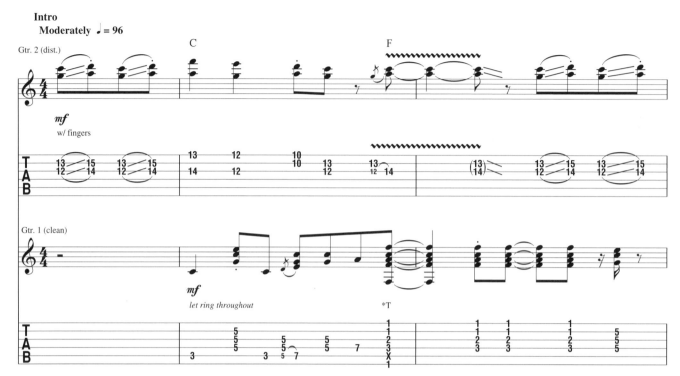

*T = Thumb on 6th string; throughout song; Gtr. 1 frets all notes
on 6th string w/ thumb.

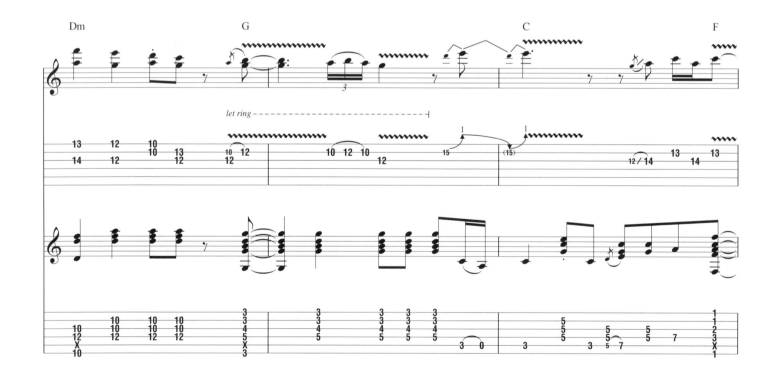

Verse

1. Had a lit - tle love ____ but I spread it ____ thin.

Fall - ing in her arms ____ and out a - gain. ____

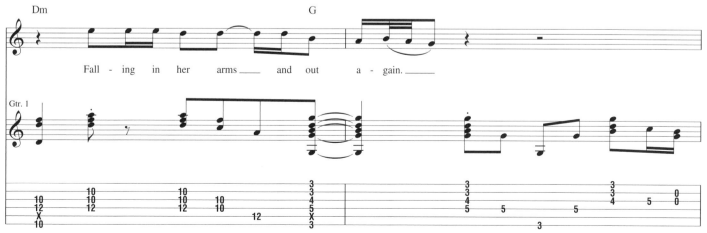

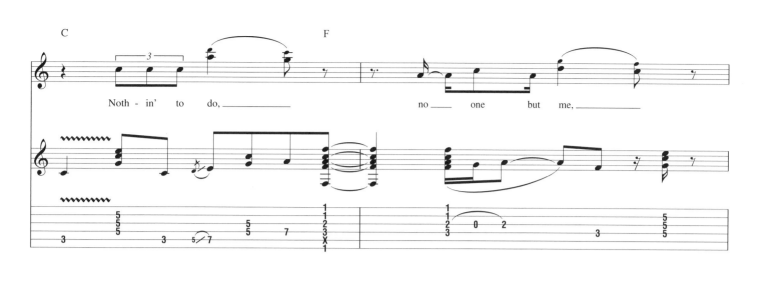

Noth - in' to do, _____ no ___ one but me, _____

and that's all I need. _____ I'm per - fect - ly lone -

𝄋 Chorus

2nd time, Gtr. 3 tacet
3rd time, Gtr. 4: w/ Fill 1

- ly. _____
ly? _____
ly. _____

I'm per - fect - ly lone -

Gtr. 1

Rhy. Fig. 1

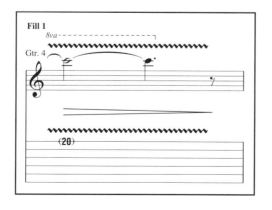

Fill 1

Gtr. 4

when their __ la - dies let 'em slip __ a - way. _____

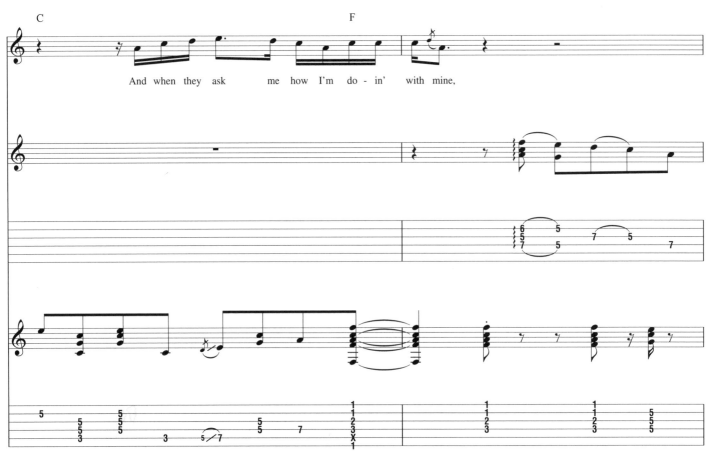

And when they ask __ me how I'm do - in' with mine,

40

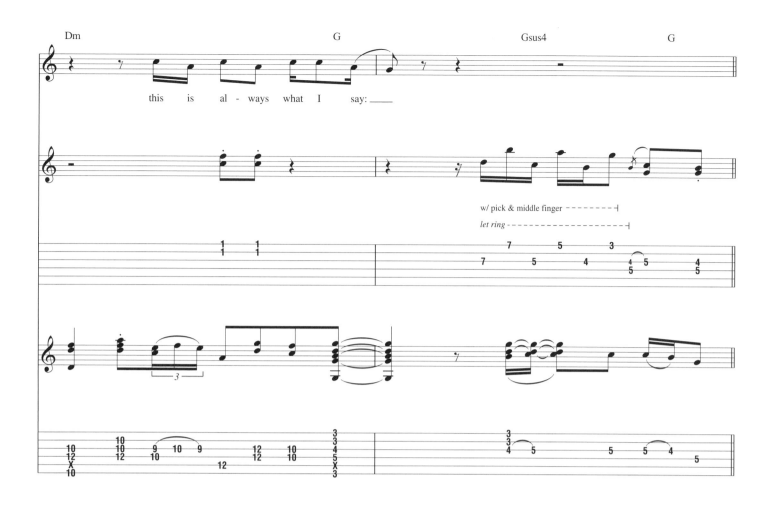

this is al - ways what I say: _____

Pre-Chorus

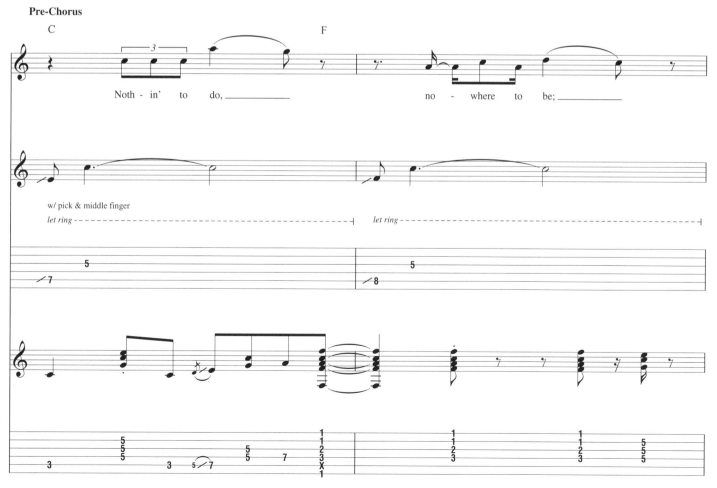

Noth - in' to do, _____ no - where to be; _____

a sim - ple lit - tle kind of free. _____

sim.

Nothin' to do, _____

no _____ one to be. _____

42

Coda 1

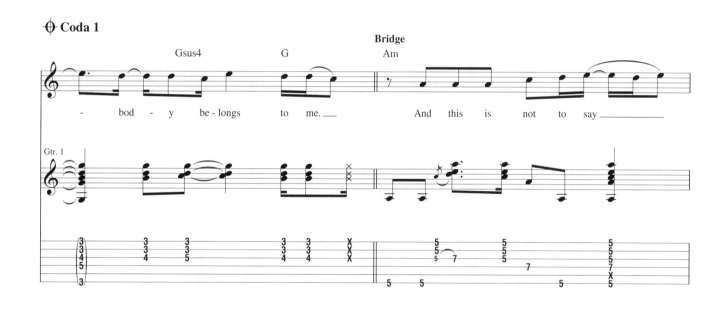

And when I look __ be-hind __ on all __ my young - er times, __

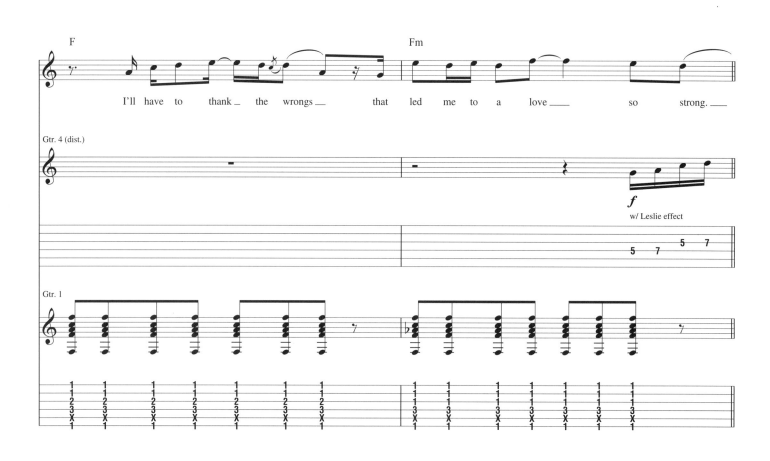

I'll have to thank __ the wrongs __ that led me to a love __ so strong. __

Gtr. 4 (dist.)

f

w/ Leslie effect

Gtr. 1

Guitar Solo

Gtr. 1: w/ Rhy. Fig. 1 (2 times)

C   F

Gtr. 4

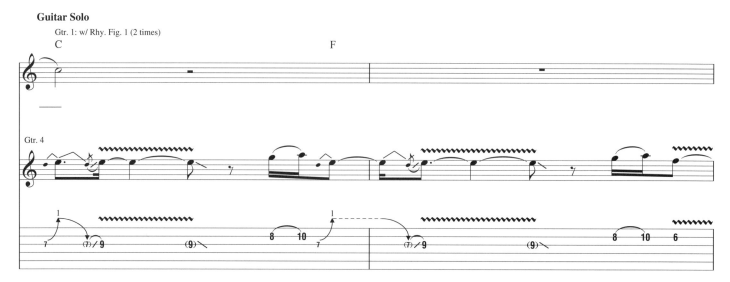

Outro

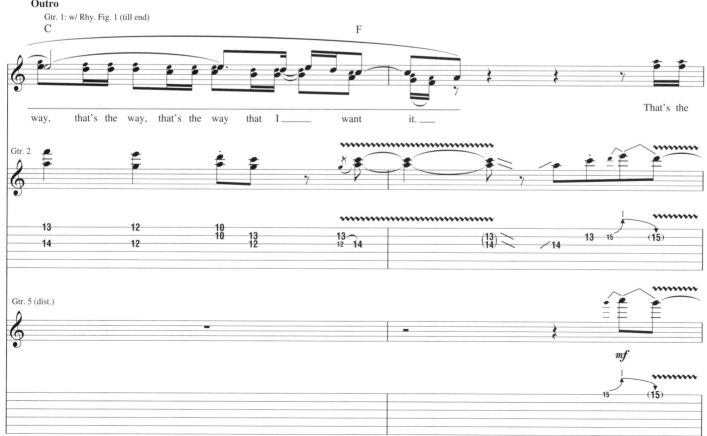

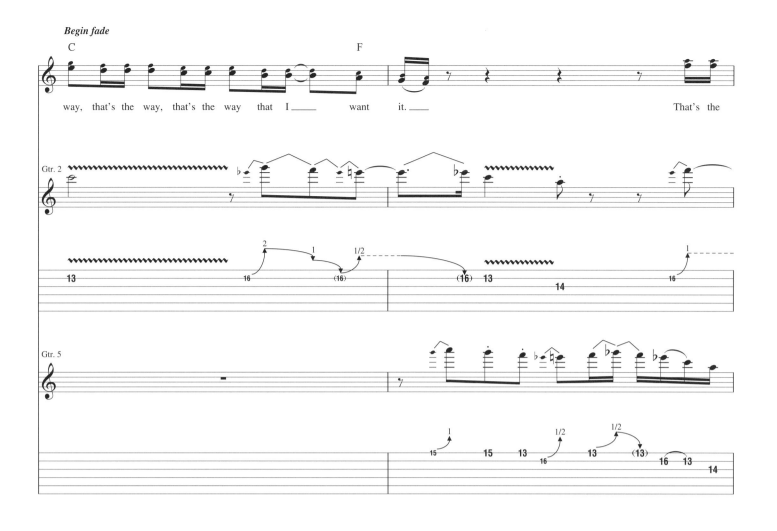

way, that's the way, that's the way that I _____ want it. _____ That's the

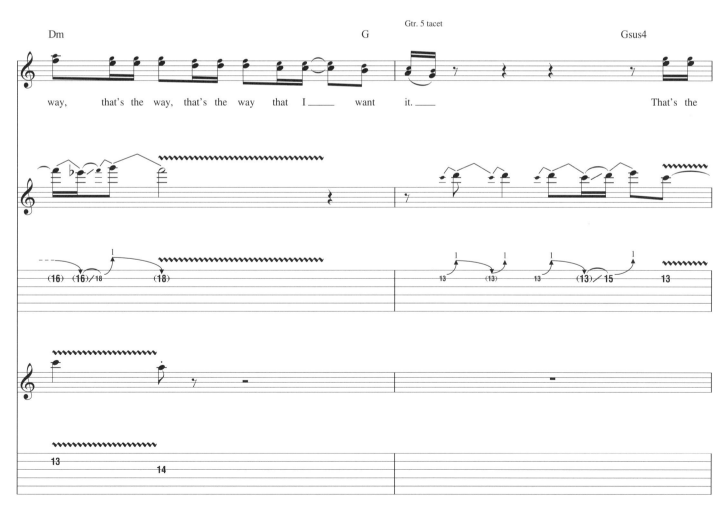

way, that's the way, that's the way that I _____ want it. _____ That's the

way, that's the way, that's the way that I ____ want it. ____ That's the

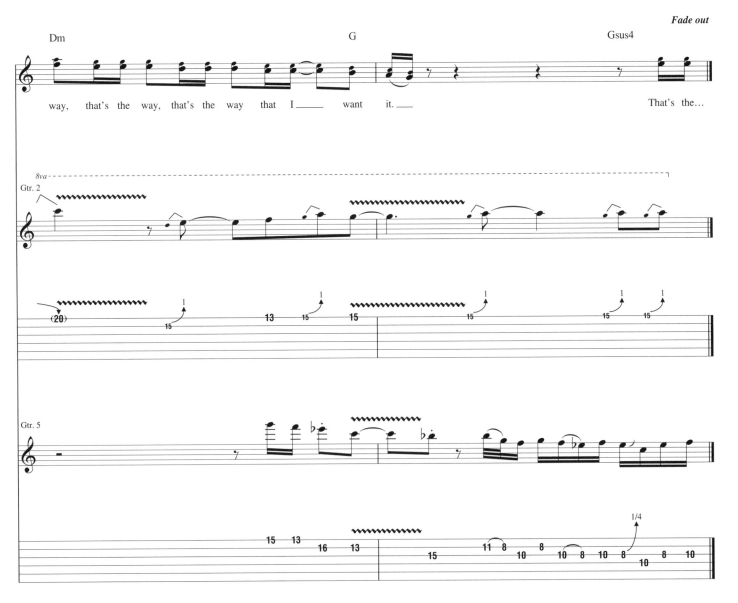

Fade out

way, that's the way, that's the way that I ____ want it. ____ That's the…

ASSASSIN

Words and Music by
John Mayer

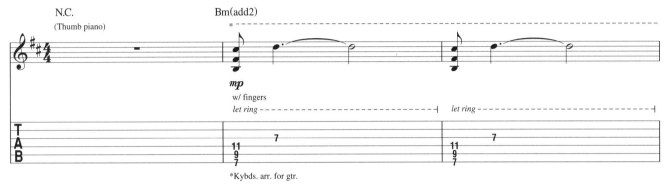

Intro

Moderately slow ♩ = 80

*Kybds. arr. for gtr.

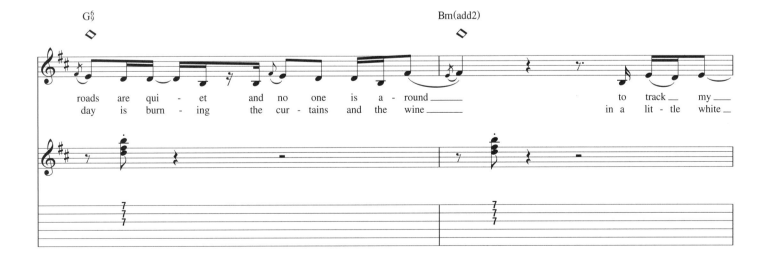

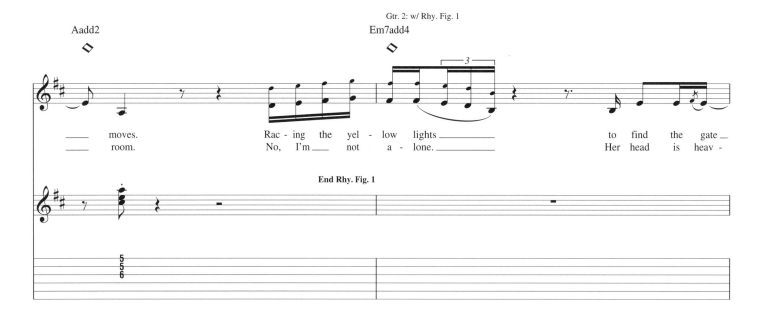

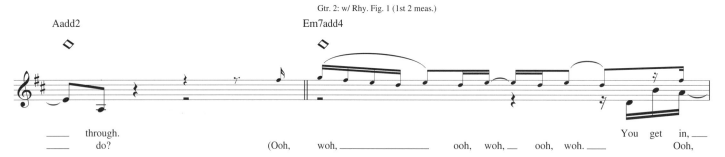

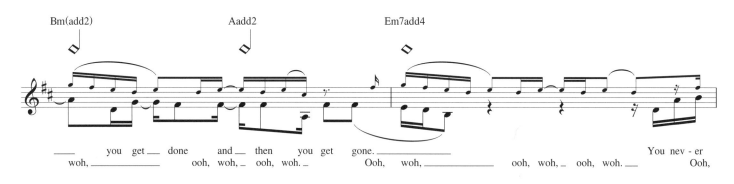

turned a - round ___ and left be - fore the sun came up a - gain, _____ but the sun ___ came
woh, _____ ooh, woh, _ ooh, woh. _ Ooh, woh, _____ ooh, woh. _____ Ooh,

|1.

Lead Voc. tacet (next 5 meas.)

up a - gain. _____
woh, _____ ooh, woh, __ ooh, woh. _____ Woh, (Hey, hey, hey, hey. ___
woh, __ ooh, woh. ___

Hey, hey, hey, hey, ___ hey. Hey, hey, hey, hey. ___
Woh, woh, __ ooh, woh.) __

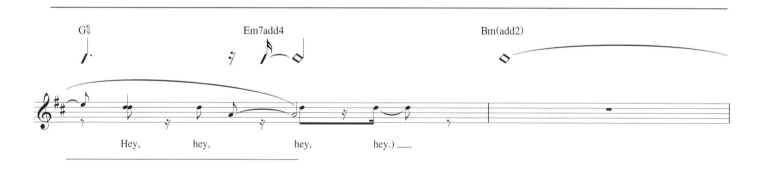

Hey, hey, hey, hey.) ___

||2.

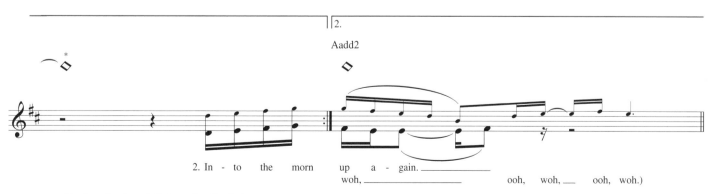

2. In - to the morn up a - gain. _____
woh, _____ ooh, woh, __ ooh, woh.)

*Starting on beat 2, gradually depress bar till end of meas.

Guitar Solo

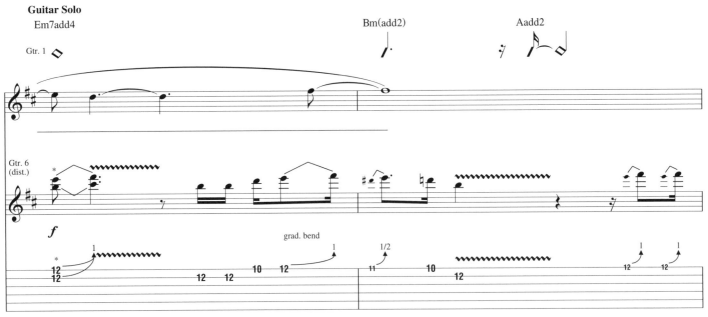

*Catch and bend both strings w/ ring finger.

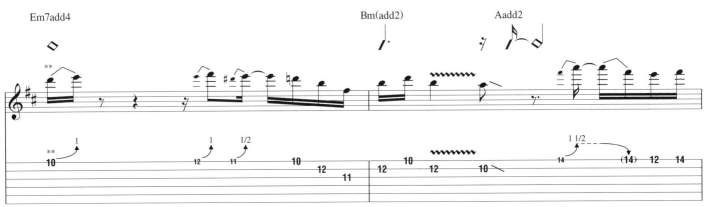

**Bend w/ 2nd finger.

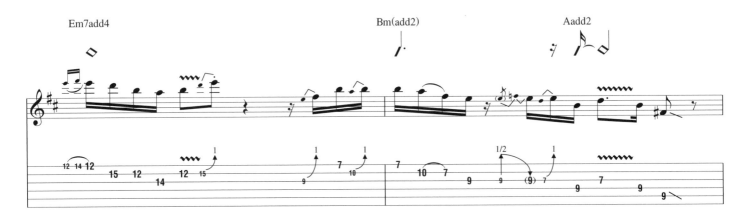

D.S. al Coda

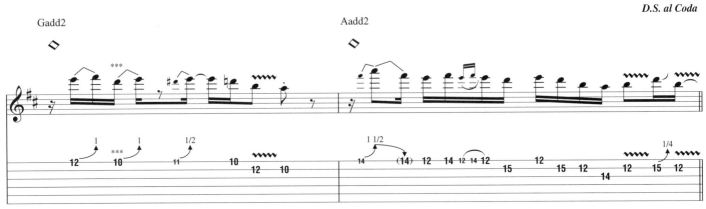

***Bend w/ 2nd finger.

CROSSROADS

Words and Music by
Robert Johnson

Intro
Moderately ♩ = 120

*Chord symbols reflect basic harmony.

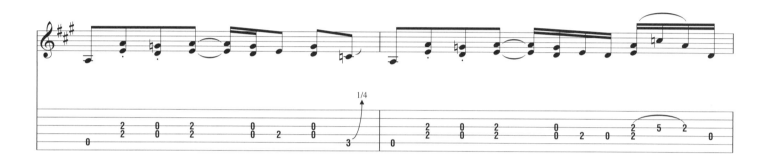

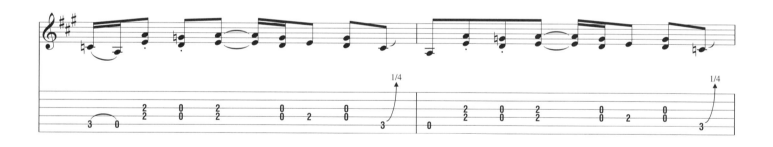

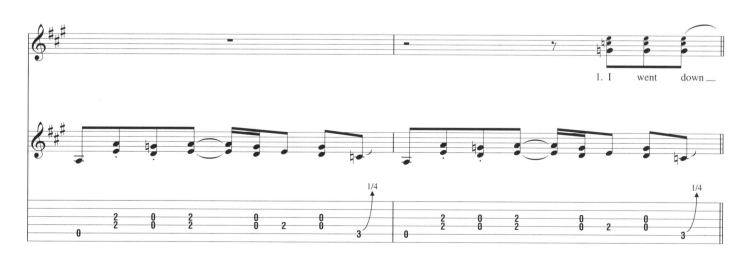

1. I went down ___

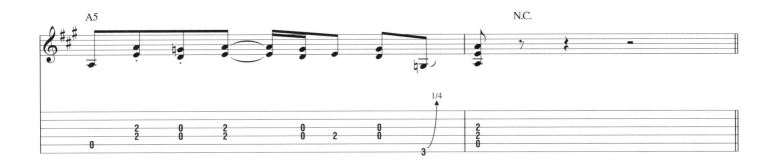

A5   N.C.

Guitar Solo

Gtr. 1: w/ Rhy. Fig. 1 (2 times)

A5   D5

Gtr. 2 (dist.)

f

w/ fingers
*w/ slight delay

*Set for quarter note regeneration w/ 1 repeat.

A5   D5

A5

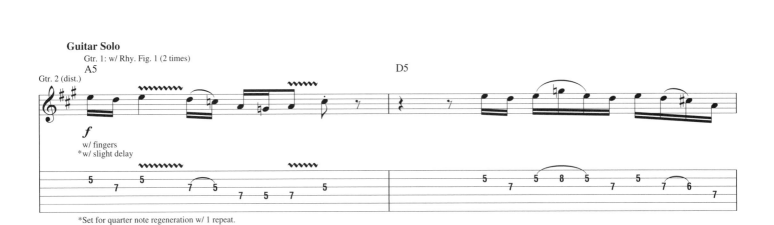

F#m   Dadd4

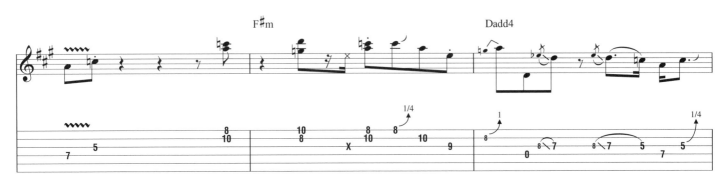

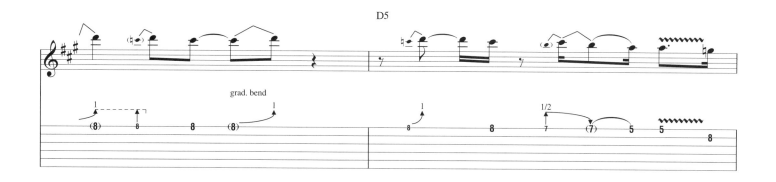

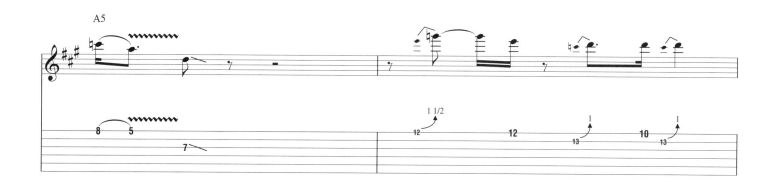

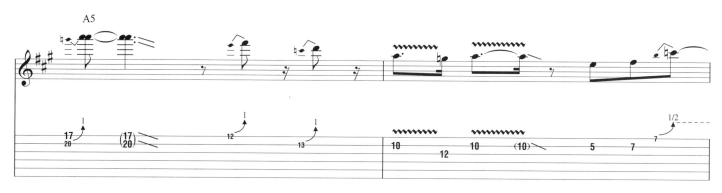

D.S. al Coda

3. You can run, ____

⊕ Coda

ing at the cross - roads; I be - lieve I'm sink - ing down. ____

WAR OF MY LIFE

Words and Music by
John Mayer

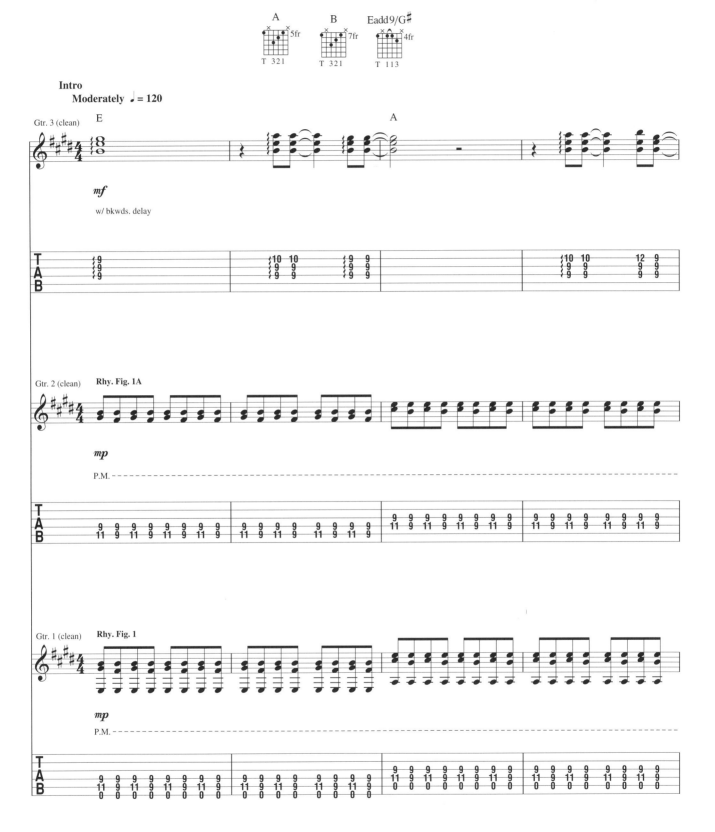

Verse

Gtrs. 1 & 2: w/ Rhy. Figs. 1 & 1A (2 times)
Gtr. 3 tacet

- gels. ___ Come out, ___ ghosts. ___ Come out, dark-

- ness; ___ bring ev-'ry-one ___ you know. ___ I'm not run-

- ing ___ and I'm not scared. ___ I am wait-

- ing ___ and well pre-pared. ___

Chorus

Gtrs. 1 & 2: w/ Rhy. Figs. 1 & 1A

I'm in the war of ___ my ___ life, ___ at the door ___ of ___ my ___ life.

64

Out of time ___ and ___ there's no - where ___ to run. ___

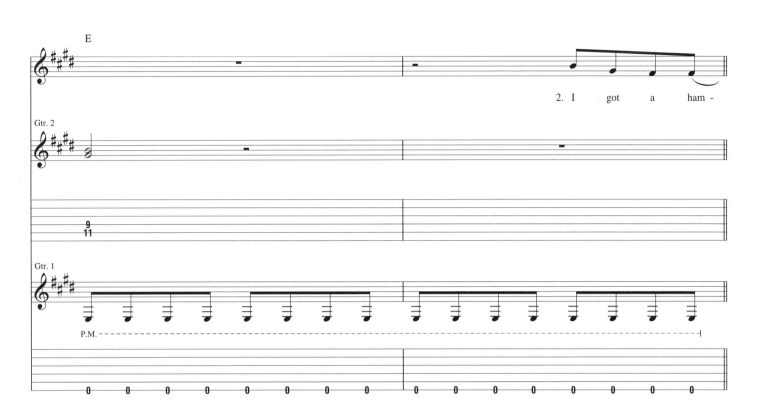

2. I got a ham -

Gtr. 2

Gtr. 1

P.M. ------

Verse

Gtrs. 1 & 2: w/ Rhy. Figs. 1 & 1A (2 times)

- mer ___ and a heart of glass. ___ I got - ta know ___

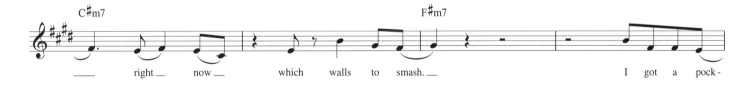

___ right ___ now ___ which walls to smash. ___ I got a pock -

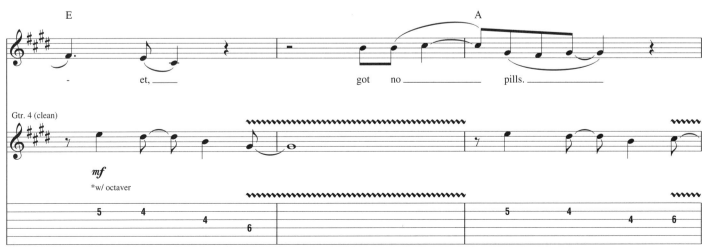

- et, ___ got no ___ pills. ___

Gtr. 4 (clean)

mf

*w/ octaver

*Set for an octave higher.

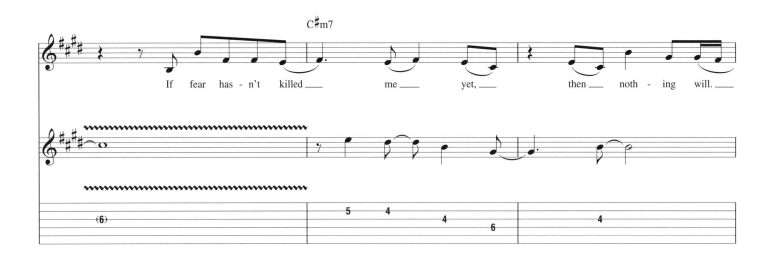

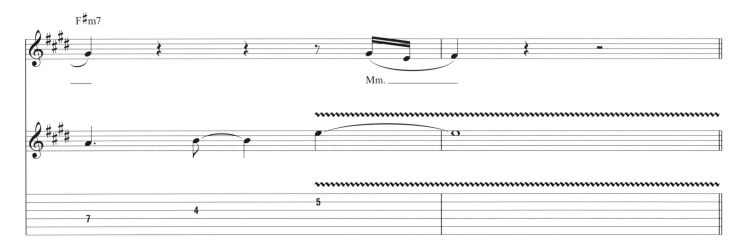

Bridge

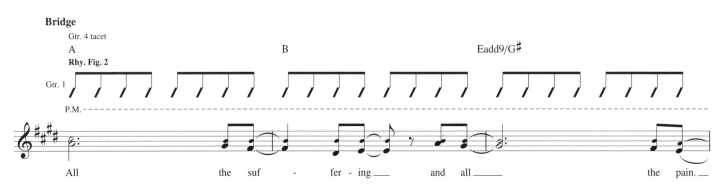

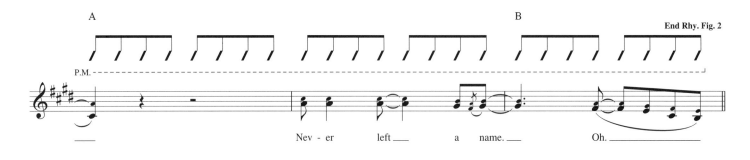

Chorus

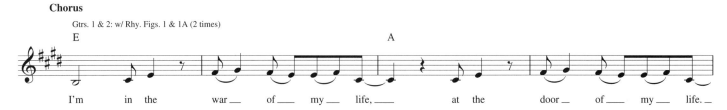

66

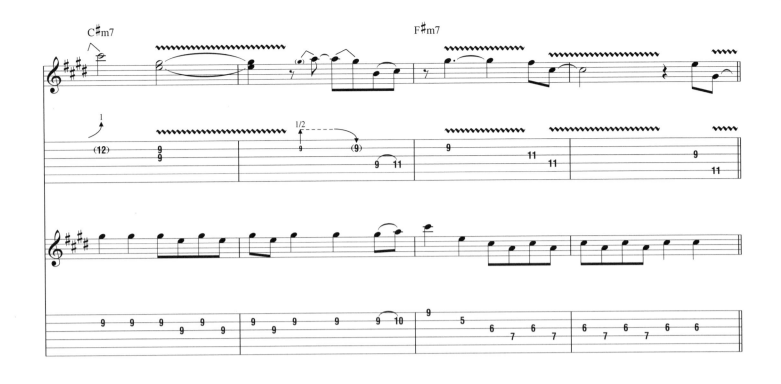

Breakdown-Chorus

Gtr. 3 tacet

I'm in the war of ___ my ___ life, ___ at the door of ___ my ___ life. ___

Gtr. 3

Gtr. 4

let ring - - - - - - - - - - - - - - - -   let ring - - - - - - - - - - - - - - - -   let ring - - -

**Gtrs. 1 & 2

P.M. -

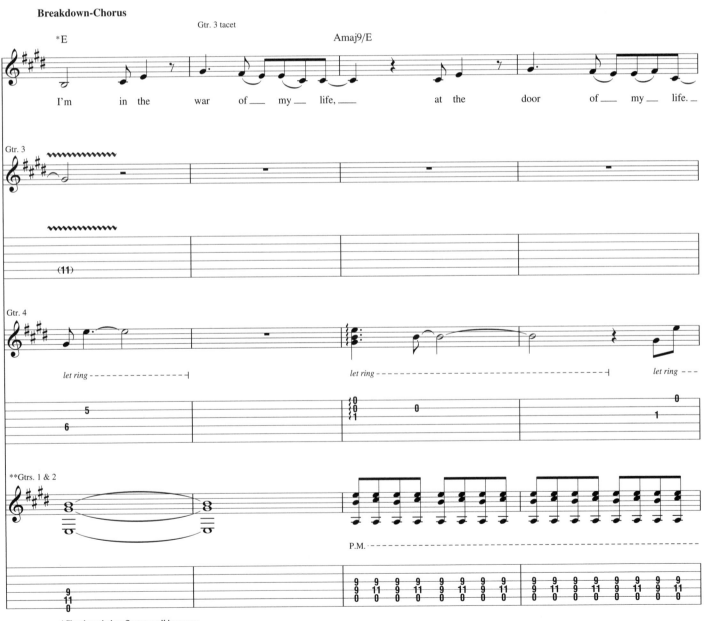

*Chord symbols reflect overall harmony.

**Composite arrangement

EDGE OF DESIRE

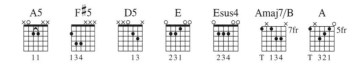

Words and Music by
John Mayer

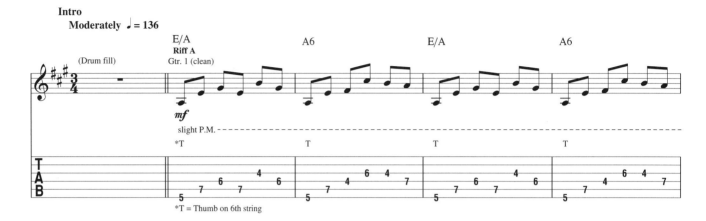

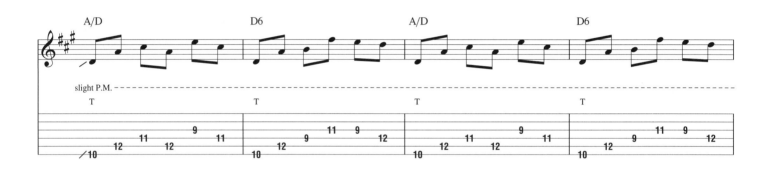

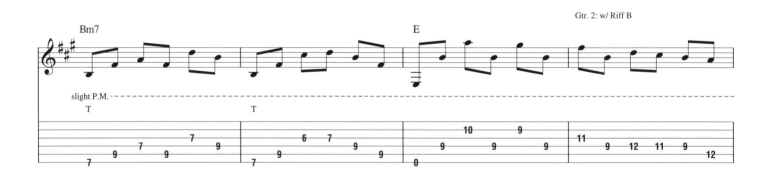

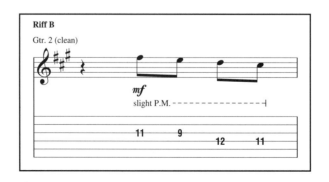

I'll go ___ back ___ on the things ___ I be - lieve. ___

There, I just ___ said ___ it. I'm scared you'll for - get ___ a - bout ___

me. ___

2. So ___

Gtr. 1

let ring - - - - - - - - - -

Riff E

End Riff E

let ring - - - - - - - - - -

Interlude

Gtr. 1: w/ Riff E (7 times)

A5

F#5

Gtr. 3 (dist.)

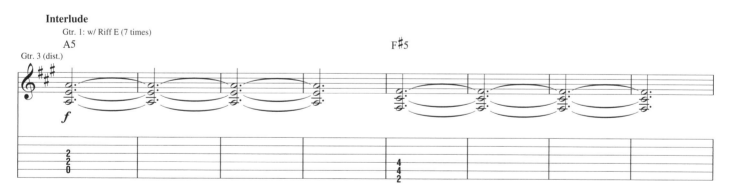

f

D5

A5

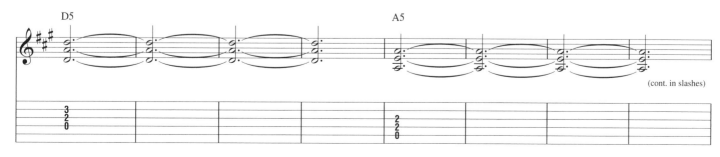

(cont. in slashes)

74

DO YOU KNOW ME

Words and Music by
John Mayer

Capo V

Intro
Moderately slow ♩ = 80

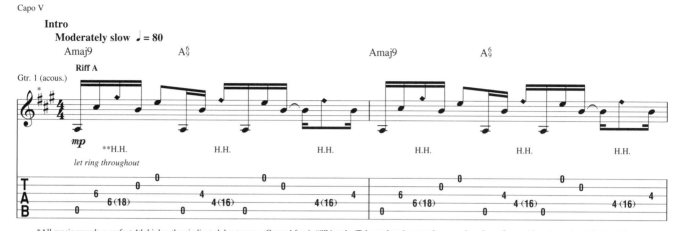

*All music sounds a perfect 4th higher than indicated due to capo. Capoed fret is "0" in tab. (Tab numbers in parentheses are imaginary fret positions located past fretboard.)

**Harp harmonics achieved by lightly touching string w/R.H. index finger at
fret indicated in parentheses and plucking w/ thumb (on bridge side of index finger).

Verse

1. It's just the strang-est ____ thing: I've seen your face some-where.

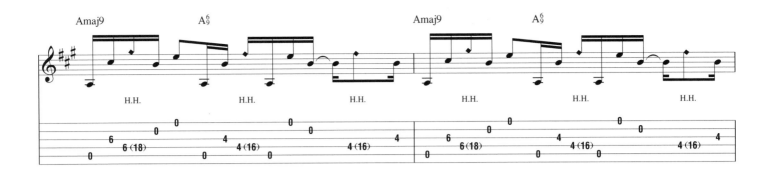

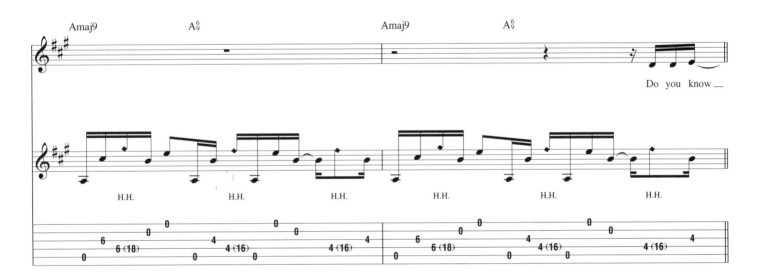

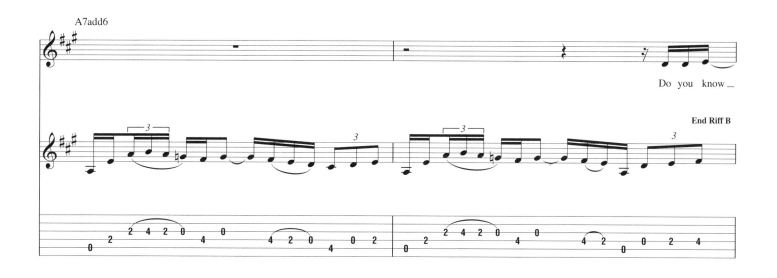

Do you know —

— me — at all?

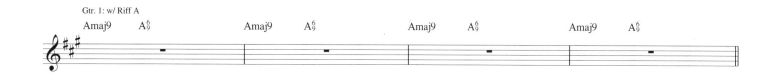

Gtr. 1: w/ Riff A

Amaj9   A⁶/₉   Amaj9   A⁶/₉   Amaj9   A⁶/₉   Amaj9   A⁶/₉

Verse

2. In all my rev - el - ry,   I thought I felt us — there.

Gtr. 1

Chorus

FRIENDS, LOVERS OR NOTHING

Words and Music by
John Mayer

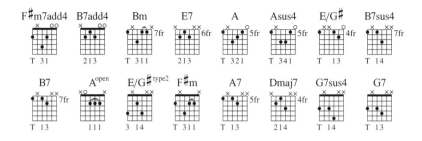

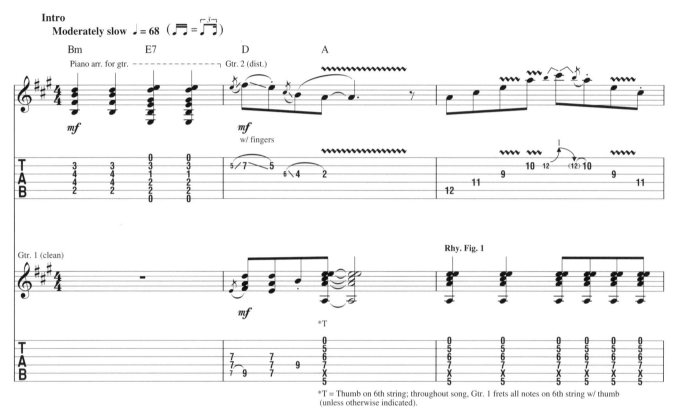

*T = Thumb on 6th string; throughout song, Gtr. 1 frets all notes on 6th string w/ thumb
(unless otherwise indicated).

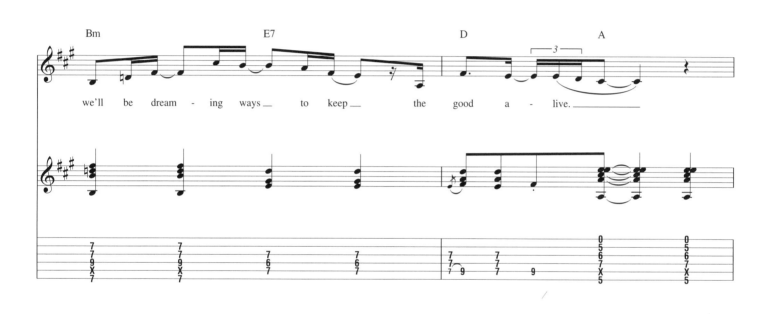

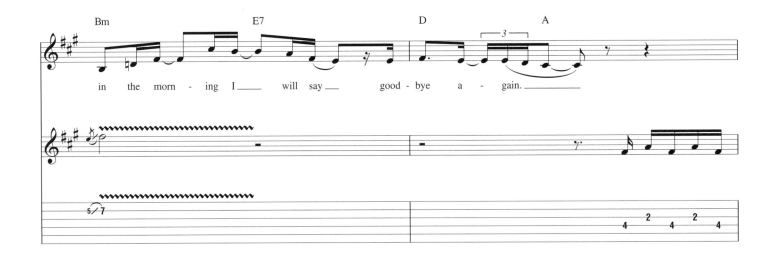

in the morn - ing I ___ will say ___ good - bye a - gain. _____

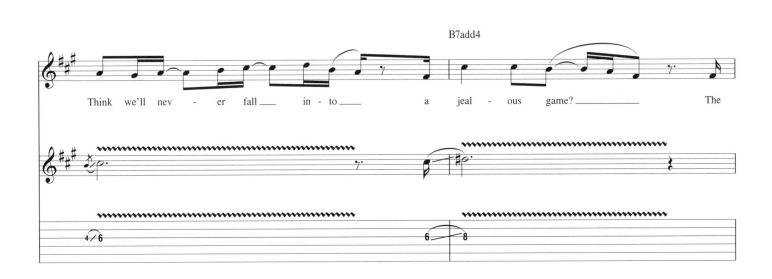

Think we'll nev - er fall ___ in - to ___ a jeal - ous game? _____ The

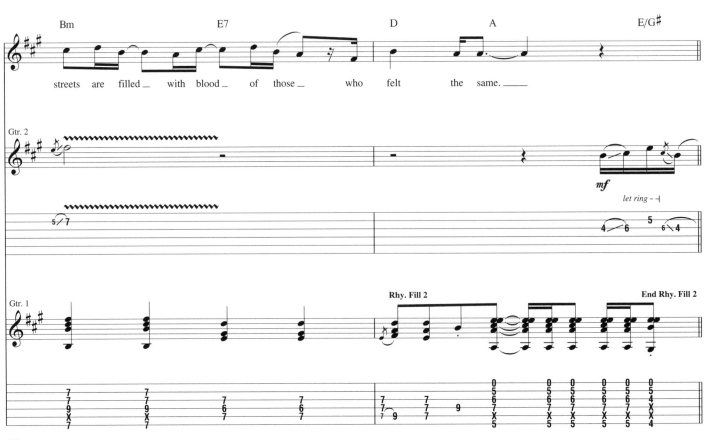

streets are filled ___ with blood ___ of those ___ who felt the same. _____

Chorus

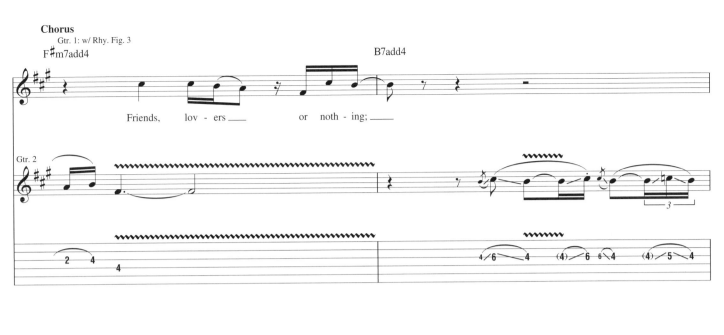

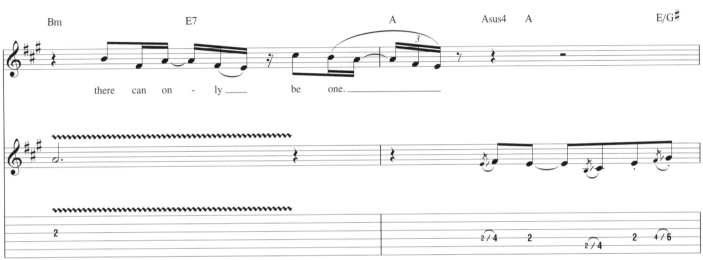

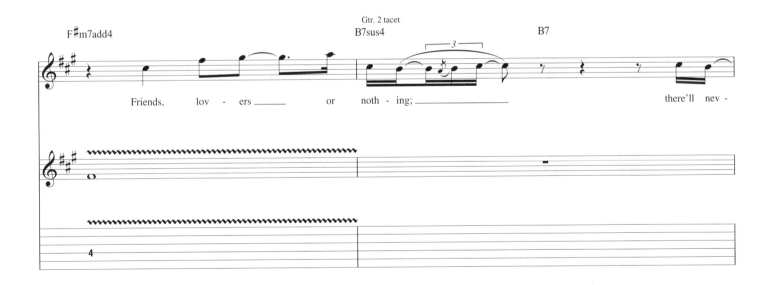

Guitar Solo

Gtr. 1: w/ Rhy. Fig. 1 (1 3/4 times)

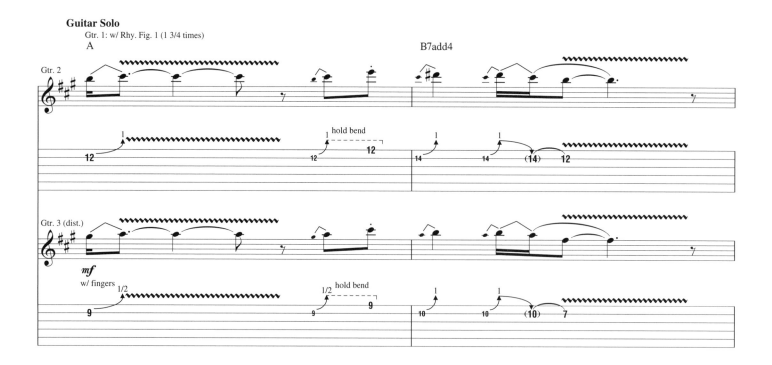

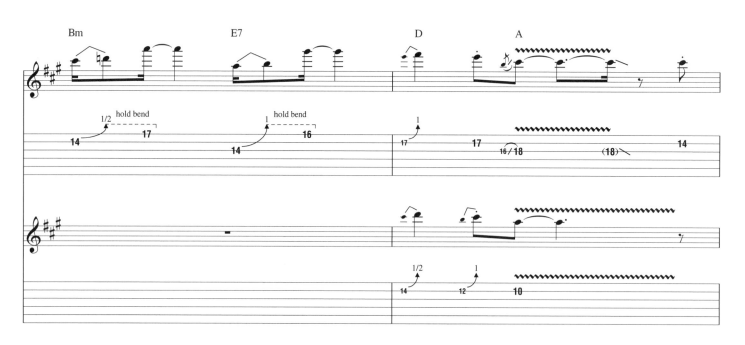

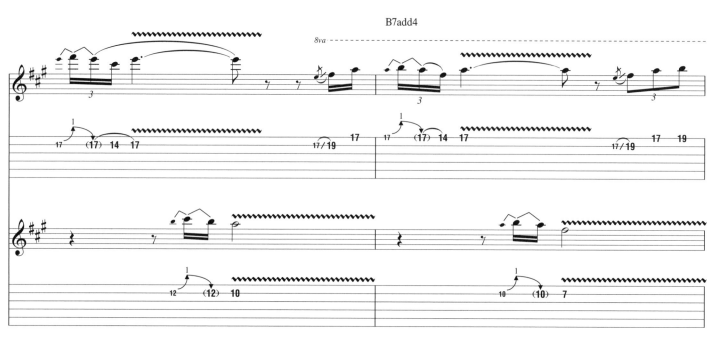

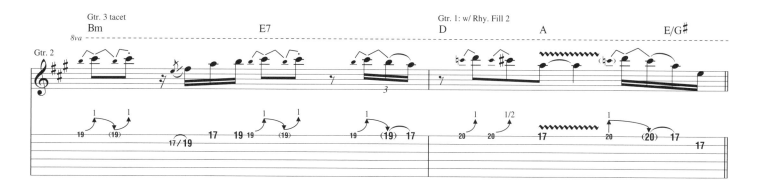

Chorus

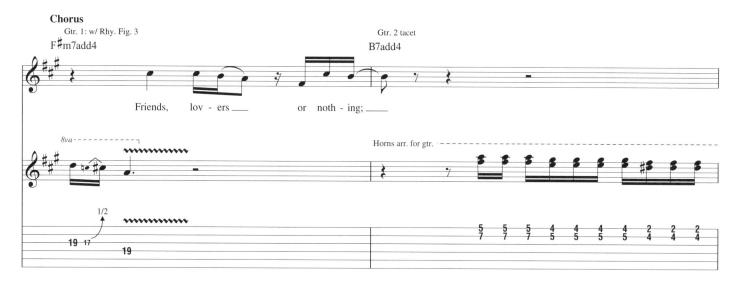

Friends, lov-ers ___ or noth-ing; ___

we can real-ly on-ly ev-er be one. ___

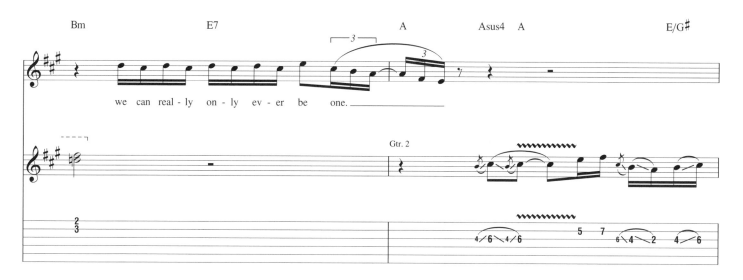

Friends, lov-ers ___ or noth-ing; ___ we'll nev-

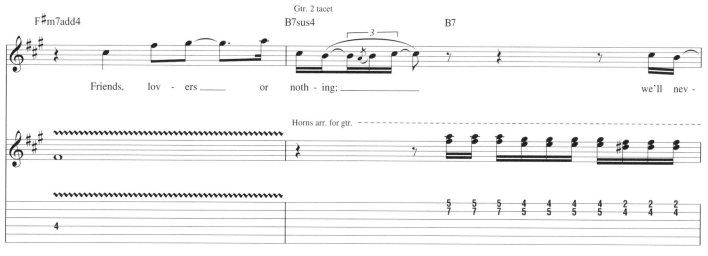

-er be ___ the in - be - tween,___ so give it up. ___

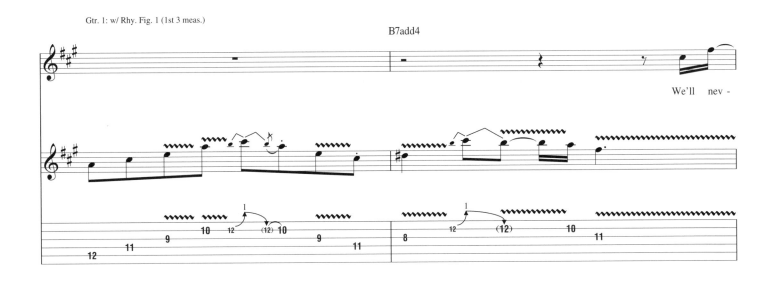

We'll nev -

-er be ___ the in - be - tween,___ so give it up. ___

*Last chord held w/ fermata.

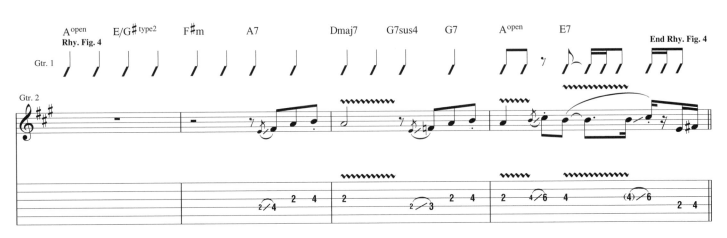

Outro

Gtr. 1: w/ Rhy. Fig. 4 (6 3/4 times)

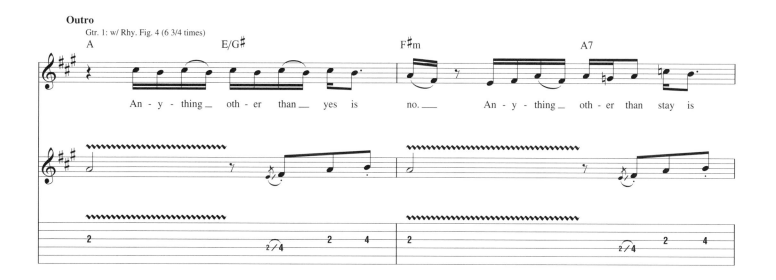

An - y - thing __ oth - er than __ yes is no. __ An - y - thing __ oth - er than stay is

go. __ An - y - thing less than "I love you" is ly - ing. __

Gtr. 2 tacet

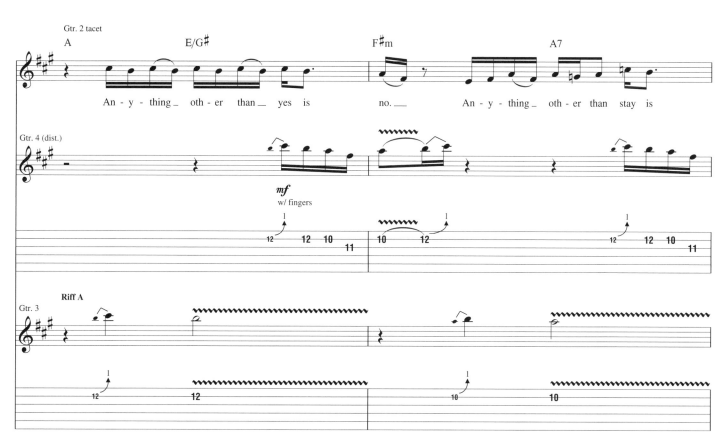

An - y - thing __ oth - er than __ yes is no. __ An - y - thing __ oth - er than stay is

Gtr. 4 (dist.)

mf
w/ fingers

Riff A

Gtr. 3

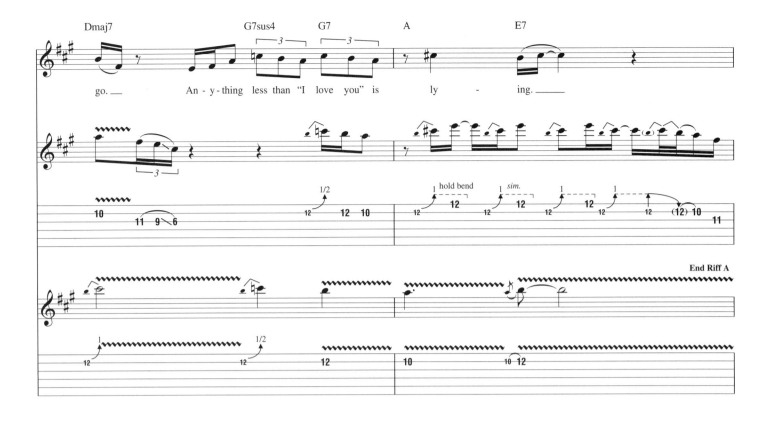

go. ___ An-y-thing less than "I love you" is ly - ing. ___

End Riff A

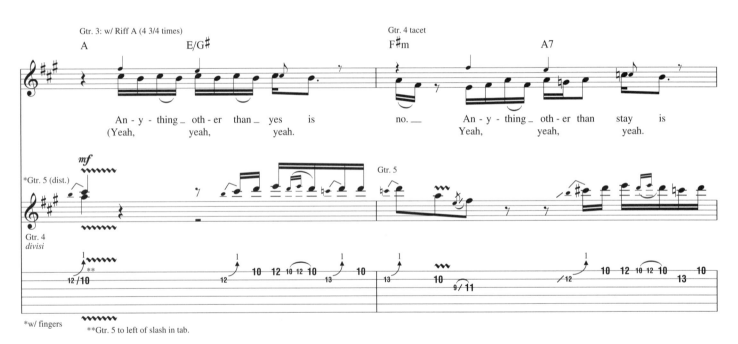

Gtr. 3: w/ Riff A (4 3/4 times)

A   E/G#   **Gtr. 4 tacet** F#m   A7

An - y-thing _ oth - er than yes is no. ___ An - y-thing _ oth - er than stay is
(Yeah,   yeah,   yeah.   Yeah,   yeah,   yeah.

*Gtr. 5 (dist.)   Gtr. 5

Gtr. 4
divisi

*w/ fingers   **Gtr. 5 to left of slash in tab.

Dmaj7   G7sus4   G7   A   E7

go. ___ An - y-thing less than "I love you" is ly - ing. ___
Yeah,   yeah,   yeah,   yeah.

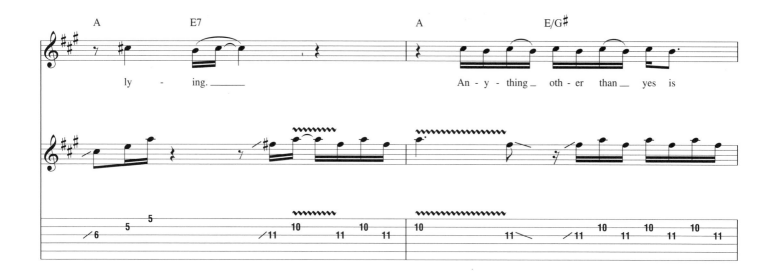

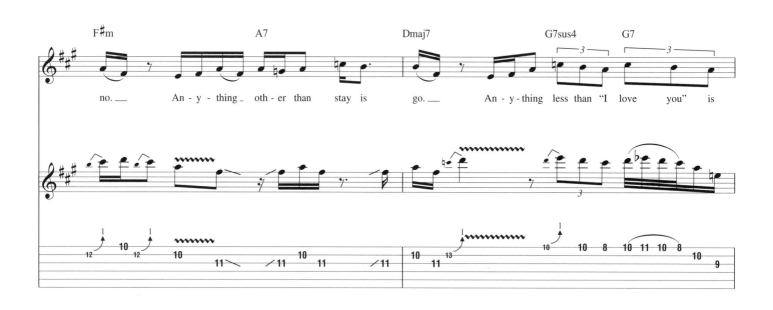

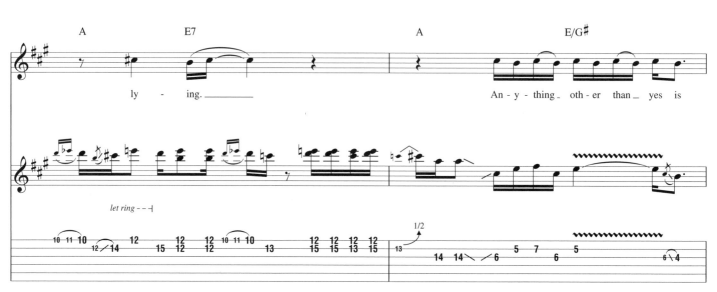

Guitar Notation Legend

Guitar music can be notated three different ways: on a *musical staff*, in *tablature*, and in *rhythm slashes*.

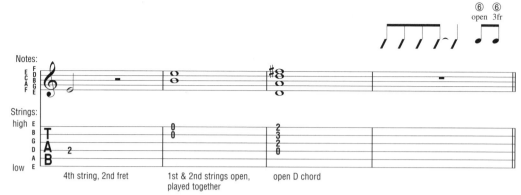

RHYTHM SLASHES are written above the staff. Strum chords in the rhythm indicated. Use the chord diagrams found at the top of the first page of the transcription for the appropriate chord voicings. Round noteheads indicate single notes.

THE MUSICAL STAFF shows pitches and rhythms and is divided by bar lines into measures. Pitches are named after the first seven letters of the alphabet.

TABLATURE graphically represents the guitar fingerboard. Each horizontal line represents a string, and each number represents a fret.

4th string, 2nd fret · 1st & 2nd strings open, played together · open D chord

---

HALF-STEP BEND: Strike the note and bend up 1/2 step.

WHOLE-STEP BEND: Strike the note and bend up one step.

GRACE NOTE BEND: Strike the note and immediately bend up as indicated.

SLIGHT (MICROTONE) BEND: Strike the note and bend up 1/4 step.

BEND AND RELEASE: Strike the note and bend up as indicated, then release back to the original note. Only the first note is struck.

PRE-BEND: Bend the note as indicated, then strike it.

VIBRATO: The string is vibrated by rapidly bending and releasing the note with the fretting hand.

WIDE VIBRATO: The pitch is varied to a greater degree by vibrating with the fretting hand.

HAMMER-ON: Strike the first (lower) note with one finger, then sound the higher note (on the same string) with another finger by fretting it without picking.

PULL-OFF: Place both fingers on the notes to be sounded. Strike the first note and without picking, pull the finger off to sound the second (lower) note.

LEGATO SLIDE: Strike the first note and then slide the same fret-hand finger up or down to the second note. The second note is not struck.

SHIFT SLIDE: Same as legato slide, except the second note is struck.

TRILL: Very rapidly alternate between the notes indicated by continuously hammering on and pulling off.

TAPPING: Hammer ("tap") the fret indicated with the pick-hand index or middle finger and pull off to the note fretted by the fret hand.

NATURAL HARMONIC: Strike the note while the fret-hand lightly touches the string directly over the fret indicated.

PINCH HARMONIC: The note is fretted normally and a harmonic is produced by adding the edge of the thumb or the tip of the index finger of the pick hand to the normal pick attack.

PICK SCRAPE: The edge of the pick is rubbed down (or up) the string, producing a scratchy sound.

MUFFLED STRINGS: A percussive sound is produced by laying the fret hand across the string(s) without depressing, and striking them with the pick hand.

PALM MUTING: The note is partially muted by the pick hand lightly touching the string(s) just before the bridge.

RAKE: Drag the pick across the strings indicated with a single motion.

TREMOLO PICKING: The note is picked as rapidly and continuously as possible.

VIBRATO BAR DIVE AND RETURN: The pitch of the note or chord is dropped a specified number of steps (in rhythm), then returned to the original pitch.

VIBRATO BAR SCOOP: Depress the bar just before striking the note, then quickly release the bar.

VIBRATO BAR DIP: Strike the note and then immediately drop a specified number of steps, then release back to the original pitch.

96